Quentin Blake

AS LARGE AS LIFE

Acknowledgements

All the pictures in this exhibition were specially created for specific hospital situations. I am enormously grateful to Steven Parissien and his colleagues for making it possible to show them in the magnificent surroundings of Compton Verney and so enable them to encounter much larger audiences.

I also have a debt of gratitude to Nick Rhodes and Stephen Barnham who, six years ago, set me off on the unexpected adventure of working for hospitals, as I have also to Ghislaine Kenyon and Patrice Marie who took the venture to France. My own team of Nikki Mansergh, Cecilia Milanesi, Liz Williams and Vicky Bingham keep the show on the road even though I lose essential correspondence amongst the drawings in the studio. And finally, though by no means least, heartfelt thanks to Claudia Zeff, who has looked after this project with characteristic calm, care and astuteness as she has others both in the past and still on their way to fruition.

This exhibition was organised by Compton Verney in collaboration with the House of Illustration

Foreword

Here at Compton Verney in seven short years we have, as an award-winning independent art gallery, established an international reputation for outstanding exhibitions that are engaging, informative and thought-provoking. Few shows have been as inspiring and life-affirming as *Quentin Blake: As Large As Life*, in which one of the nation's foremost illustrators addresses important social and healthcare issues with typical sensitivity, humour and deftness. Quentin Blake's recent series of pictures for hospitals generate a fitting synergy with our ambition to share both historic and contemporary art with as many people as possible.

We are delighted to have worked with Quentin Blake on this fascinating exhibition, which after being displayed at Compton Verney will tour to The Foundling Museum, Paisley Museum, Laing Art Gallery and Kirkby Gallery. We hope you will enjoy the works illustrated in this accompanying book as much as we have.

Dr Steven Parissien
Director, Compton Verney

As large as life

It was a moment I won't forget – in the first year of the 21st century, as it happens – when Michael Wilson, at that time Director of Exhibitions at the National Gallery, invited me to draw on its walls. I had no idea at the time, however, that it was my first step into a decade in which my people escaped from the pages of books, where they had been disporting themselves for the past forty years, and got bigger.

In fact I did not, properly speaking, draw on the walls of the National Gallery. The occasion was an exhibition called *Tell Me A Picture* that I had proposed as part of the activities of my two-year stint as the first Children's Laureate. The drawings guided you round the exhibition, and were actually drawn in the studio and printed, enlarged to life-size, on transparent acetate which could easily be applied to the Gallery walls, as though drawn there, and as easily stripped off afterwards. The fact that modern techniques of printing have the capability of enlarging a drawing to any size with extraordinary fidelity to the original opened up all kinds of possibilities, including, if necessary, drawings as large as life, or larger.

The National Gallery exhibition was followed by one at the Petit Palais, which is the art museum of the city of Paris, and where drawings of updated cherubs flew high on the walls above the chosen paintings. In due course I put my name to a drawing big enough to wrap a building. The original was perhaps 20 × 30 inches, but what the passengers arriving at St Pancras station saw was five storeys high.

This is the printing technology that makes the present exhibition possible – all the pictures in the show are digital prints, which seem to be known in English as giclée prints (though strangely not in France). The use of this technique in the hospital projects I have worked on has a number of advantages. A significant one to the hospital is that the costs are relatively low, compared with original works. I am simply paid for the right to reproduce the pictures, which I keep; and the insurance cost, of something that is replaceable, is correspondingly low.

From the series *You’re Only Young Twice*, Kershaw Ward,
South Kensington and Chelsea Mental Health Centre

From the series *You're Only Young Twice*, Kershaw Ward, South Kensington and Chelsea Mental Health Centre

None of the pictures would have come into existence if it had not been for the Nightingale Project. This is a scheme to get art and music into hospitals and is the initiative of Stephen Barnham and Dr Nick Rhodes. Another moment that I won't forget was when, in December 2005, they invited me to produce a set of pictures for the refurbished Kershaw Ward in South Kensington and Chelsea Mental Health Centre. It was for residential elderly patients; the fact that the day of our meeting was coincidentally my birthday seemed to underline the fact that I had an added age qualification. That first set of pictures doesn't appear in this exhibition, except as a book. Once my French publisher Christine Baker at Gallimard had seen the pictures she identified a publishing opportunity: they became *Vive Nos Vieux Jours* which in its turn became *You're Only Young Twice*, and in due course similar titles in several other languages. This venture led on to others, and it is samples from four of them that you see in this exhibition.

Quentin Blake

Our friends in the circus

This set of prints was produced for an older adults mental health ward at Northwick Park Hospital, Harrow. It came about because at one stage we were talking about producing a sequence of works for a hospital which happened to be in Circus Road, London (although that is not where the pictures are now). The circus analogy spoke to me immediately and I wanted to show that my fellow seniors – clowns, jugglers, tightrope walkers – could still produce wonders of agility and balance even if in a restrained fashion. Nothing especially restrained about the fire-eater, I admit; and I have the impression that it is one of the most popular of the prints, perhaps because of its open defiance of any consideration of Health and Safety.

Ordinary life in Vincent Square

The Vincent Square Clinic in London is for people with eating disorders; some of them are resident and some outpatients.

One of the most interesting aspects for me of these hospital projects is in attempting to understand the situation of the patients involved and imagining the kind of drawings which might be appropriate. The Circus pictures are meant to be amusing and a distraction, while at the same time optimistic about the people who will be looking at them. After talking to some of the patients and the staff at Vincent Square it seemed to me that what they needed was pictures of ordinary everyday life, relaxed and congenial.

As you see the pictures in this exhibition, away from the hospital, I think they might seem to have no reference to the circumstances of the patients whose walls they decorate; but in fact the acknowledgement is present – I hope discreetly enough not to seem like nagging.

Mothers and babies underwater

I worked with Ghislaine Kenyon on both my National Gallery and Petit Palais exhibitions. It was thanks to her and her contact with Patrice Marie and his experience at the French Ministry of Culture that I was commissioned to produce a sequence of pictures for the Hôpital Armand Trousseau, the children's hospital in Paris.

It was while we were discussing that project there was mention of a possible maternity department commission. Although this project never materialised, the thought of producing something for a maternity department never left my head. My ideas came to fruition at the new maternity hospital, part of the Centre Hospitalier Universitaire in Angers, France.

It is sometimes difficult to know where ideas originate. The sequence of pictures I drew for the Gordon Hospital, which are of fully clothed everyday people swimming underwater: where did they come from? And how was it that a related sequence provided the maternity solution? If I try to think about it, there seem sometimes to have been periods of a sort of absent-mindedness when ideas think of themselves. At any rate, the Angers mothers and babies are swimmers. I was aware of amniotic fluid, and that newborn babies can, at least for a while, swim naturally. Later my friends at Angers noted an extra appropriateness in that their hospital is on the bank of the river Maine, which has been known to flood its banks.

These swimmers are absolutely unclothed, surrounded by trails of seaweed in decorative Rococo swirls. In former times young women appeared nude in paintings with the excuse that they were classical – they were nymphs and goddesses and suchlike. These Angers mothers and babies are real, but the places where the pictures appear are private and, although real, they appear in a parallel world where their swimming expresses and celebrates, I hope, their new-found liberty after the pains of labour.

The enthusiasm which the doctors and midwives manifested for this project was, for me, really supportive and motivating. I remember an observation from M. Vapaille who had administrative control of the scheme: "The important thing" he said (as I waited for some crucial financial consideration to be revealed) "is the exchange of look between the mother and the baby."

There is a single colour for each image, mostly underwater greens and blues, added to the figures and seaweed only, onto already wet paper. The movement of water is only shown on the bodies, not on the water itself. They just might even be flying.

Welcome to Planet Zog

After I had completed the pictures that made up *You're Only Young Twice* for the Nightingale Project, Nick Rhodes and Stephen Barnham invited me to do something similar for a young audience – this time for the children and young people's health centre in Alexandra Avenue in South Harrow.

One of the things that I find attractive about illustration is that there is always the possibility of fantasy and metaphor (when the moment is right – you will have noticed that there is nothing like that in the Vincent Square pictures). So this set of pictures takes place on Planet Zog, where the alien creatures may have bandaged fingers or depressive problems or your consultant may be green and have extra arms, which I hope is not necessarily a disadvantage.

As in one or two other projects, a lot happens up trees, here strange striped ones; and the consequence of this, apart from its decorative function, is that everything is happening at the same distance from the spectator. This was particularly useful in the banner that hangs in the big waiting room at Alexandra Avenue. The observation that I most value was from the person who said, "If you had to wait long enough you might get cured before you got to your appointment."

I am sure that art in hospitals must have a sustaining, reassuring and even perhaps an uplifting effect. The added characteristic of these schemes is that they are directed at a specific audience of patients (and, of course, of staff and specialists). In the hospitals the pictures are simply housed in very shallow acrylic boxes (as they are in this exhibition) so that, although they are not murals, they are flat on the walls. What we are looking at is, effectively, illustrated walls.

Quentin Blake and the Nightingale Project

The Nightingale Project is a charity which brightens up mental health hospitals through the arts. A generation ago the value of art in hospitals was not widely understood, but it is now increasingly accepted that if the buildings in which medical treatment takes place can be made less clinical and more human, less daunting and more welcoming, then something important will have been achieved: in other words the environment can contribute to the healing process.

The Nightingale Project was founded in 1998 at South Kensington and Chelsea Mental Health Centre, where I was working as a Clinical Psychologist. My view was that in Mental Health in particular, it was absurd and counter-productive to try to offer therapy in a depressing environment, and felt that to bring life and colour into the wards and waiting areas would lift the spirits in a helpful way. Through temporary exhibitions, through installing art for permanent display, and through live music, we set about humanising the environment, and were very struck by the patients' response. In our outpatients' area in 2008, we put on an exhibition of lithographs originally produced for the Lyons Corner Houses in the 1940s and 50s. During this show I was startled to hear a patient who had come in to see a psychiatrist about her depression exclaim, after looking at the pictures, "I will be going home feeling *inspired!*" Similarly, after a performance by a ukulele player on one of the wards, the manager, commenting on the way that emotionally withdrawn patients had come to life, said, "It's better than *any* medication!"

When, in 2005, Kershaw Ward, the acute ward for older people at the Centre, was undergoing a major refurbishment, some new art was requested to adorn the walls of the ward when it reopened. We felt that it would be good to have pictures which communicated a positive view of ageing, so Stephen Barnham, one of the directors of the Nightingale Project, suggested approaching Quentin Blake and inviting him to produce a set of pictures of older people enjoying themselves. Luckily for us, Quentin leapt at the chance to do this, feeling perhaps that having worked primarily for a very young audience, this afforded him an unusual opportunity to work for people closer to his own age. The result was a remarkably vital set of drawings, imbued with Quentin's characteristically light, compassionate humour, of older people dancing, lifting weights, playing the double bass, or even swinging from the branches of a tree. The pictures abundantly fulfilled the brief that Quentin had been given, and entirely succeeded in creating a cheerful and uplifting mood for the inpatients, staff and visitors. The most common comments

heard from patients about the Kershaw pictures are "They make me smile" "They make me laugh" – and that, in a psychiatric hospital, is a significant achievement.

Having had such an invigorating effect on the atmosphere in one ward, Quentin was enthusiastic to experiment further in this area. The Nightingale Project works with Central and North West London NHS Foundation Trust, whose premises are spread across a large swathe of the capital. Consequently, while at the same time working on projects with various other artists, we have been able to collaborate in a hugely rewarding way with Quentin on several further sites in the Trust. In addition, we have seen him spiral outwards, as it were, to maternity hospitals in north-east England and western France, and a children's hospital in Paris – surprising, amusing and inspiring thousands of hospital patients along the way. It has been a privilege to be part of that journey.

Dr Nick Rhodes, Director, Nightingale Project
www.nightingaleproject.org

The pictures for Planet Zog were drawn with a Waverley nib and Indian ink, on Arches Fin watercolour paper; those for Our friends in the circus with reed pens and those for Vincent Square with quills, on the same paper. The Angers pictures were drawn with reed pens on Canson watercolour paper. The colour throughout is watercolour.

Published by Compton Verney 2011 on the occasion of the exhibition
Quentin Blake: As Large As Life
Compton Verney, 15 October – 11 December 2011

ISBN no: 978-0-9552719-6-0

Designed by Anne Odling-Smee, O-SB Design
Printed by Deckers Snoeck, Antwerp

Compton Verney
Warwickshire
CV35 9HZ

T. 01926 645 500
www.comptonverney.org.uk
Registered charity no. 1032478

Supported by

PETER MOORES FOUNDATION